ENGINEERING POWER!

MACHINES AT SEA

Kay Barnham

Gareth Stevens
PUBLISHING

Please visit our website, www.garethstevens.com. For a free color catalog of all our high-quality books, call toll free 1-800-542-2595 or fax 1-877-542-2596.

Cataloging-in-Publication Data

Names: Barnham, Kay.
Title: Machines at sea / Kay Barnham.
Description: New York : Gareth Stevens Publishing, 2023. | Series: Engineering power! | Includes glossary and index.
Identifiers: ISBN 9781538277539 (pbk.) | ISBN 9781538277553 (library bound) | ISBN 9781538277546 (6pack) | ISBN 9781538277560 (ebook)
Subjects: LCSH: Ships--Juvenile literature. | Boats and boating--Juvenile literature. | Submarines--Juvenile literature.
Classification: LCC VM150.B376 2023 | DDC 623.82--dc23

Published in 2023 by
Gareth Stevens Publishing
29 E. 21st Street
New York, NY 10010

Editor: Elise Short
Design and illustration: Collaborate

Picture Credits
Alamy: Archivah 24b; DFID 23t; Ian Fairbrother 7t. Buquebus.com: 15b. Dreamstime: Johnnydao 11t; Georgios Kollidas 5t. Enata.com: 13b. Getty Images: Stocktrek Images 17b. MercMarine.com: 9b. Nuytco.com: 27b. Shutterstock: Peter Abel 29b; Stanislaw Bozek 28b; brillenstimmer 10b; Ron Ellis 29t; jennyt 20t; YM.Ku Shahril 22t; Roberto Sorin 28t. Theflyship.com: 21t. Nick Verola/Shamina Abas/Tritonsubs.com: 24t. US Navy Photo:MC2 Ridge Leoni 16t. Wikimedia Commons: Drents Museum musealndrenthe.nl CC 8b; Government of Canada employee PD 12t; John Webber published 1784 PD 15t. Zapata.com 19t.

Printed in the United States of America

CPSIA compliance information: Batch #CSGS23: For further information contact Gareth Stevens, New York, New York at 1-800-542-2595.

Contents

WHAT DO ENGINEERS DO?

Engineers use science, technology and math to find ways of doing countless different things. So whether it's whizzing around the world, diving beneath the waves, tunneling under the seabed or zooming to the moon, it's engineers who make that happen.

MACHINES IN THE SEA

Often, engineers design and build a machine to do a certain job such as help us to navigate the sea. But before engineers can even start work, they have to know exactly what that machine will need to do. Will it skim across the waves to transport cargo fast? Or will it explore the seabed to find minerals? Will it be powered by an engine or the wind? Does it need to carry passengers or heavy cargo? Once they have the answers to these questions—and many more—they can begin!

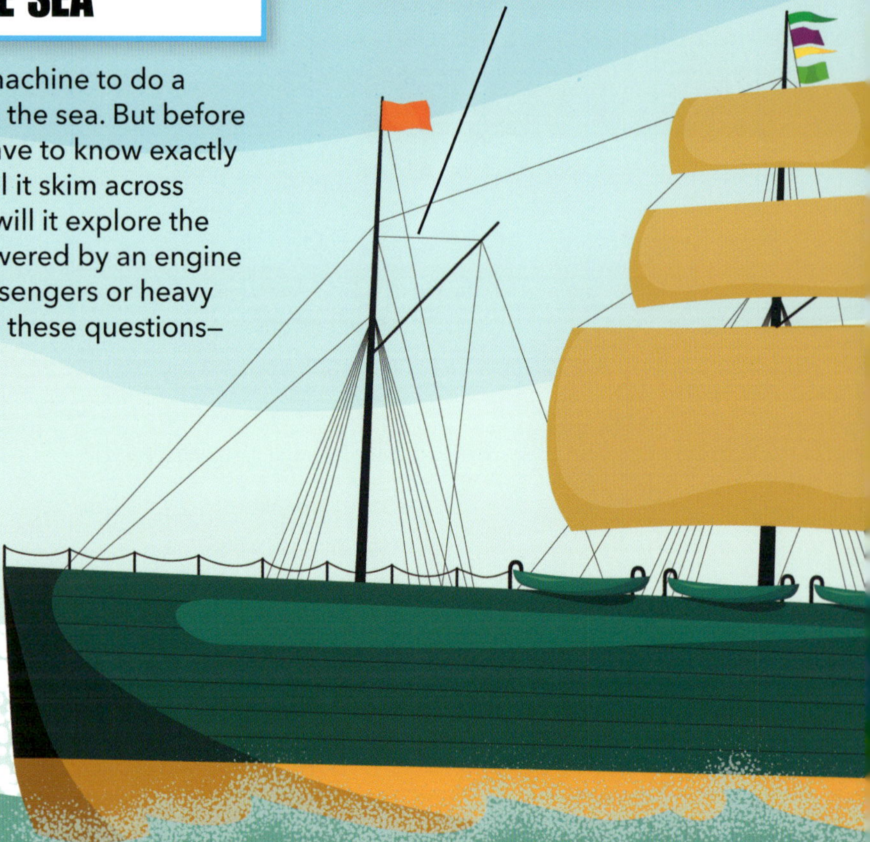

The rigging is the ropes and cables that support and control the sails.

HOW BOATS FLOAT

It doesn't matter if they are sailing boats, fishing boats, dragon boats, steamboats or speed boats, it's the same science that explains how boats—and ships—float.

When a boat floats, it displaces water. This simply means that when the boat sits in water, some water is pushed out of the way. There's no longer room for it because the boat is there instead. If the weight of the boat is the same as the displaced water, it floats!

The water itself also helps the boat to float. Water pushes upwards against an object and the deeper the water, the greater the pressure. This is called buoyant force.

Famous engineer Isambard Kingdom Brunel designed the SS Great Eastern, a massive, iron paddle steamer. When it was launched in 1858, it was the largest ship in the world. But, even though it was so big and heavy, it floated because its weight was the same as the weight of the water it displaced.

Funnels let out steam and smoke from the boilers.

Masts are large poles that carry the rigging for the sails.

SS Great Eastern was the first ship to have a double hull (one inside the other). If it hit a reef, this made it far less likely to sink than a single-hulled ship.

SS Great Eastern was so big that it needed both a paddle wheel and a screw propeller to power it. The paddle wheel was 49 feet (15 m) in diameter and was powered by steam boilers. The propeller was 26 feet (8 m) in diameter.

The Plimsoll is a line marked on the side of a ship to show the maximum load that it can carry. If the Plimsoll line is lower than the waterline, the ship is overloaded and in danger of sinking.

Turn the page to find out all about other magnificent machines at sea that engineering power has made possible ...

SHIPS

Hundreds of years ago, ships sailed on voyages of discovery. Now, even though other, faster types of transport have been invented, ships are still very important. Merchant ships are used to efficiently transport most of the world's cargo. Passenger ships carry passengers and vacationers across the sea. They are also used for defence and research.

LOADS AND LOADS

Oil, grain, iron ore, sugar, salt and books are just a few of the millions of things that are transported by sea. Although ships travel slowly, they are built to carry very heavy cargoes, so they can carry a lot of goods at the same time. This means that shipping is much cheaper than taking things by airplane. Today, over 50,000 merchant ships are used to transport goods around the world.

Different types of merchant ship carry different types of load. Tankers carry large cargoes of liquid or gas. Meanwhile, container ships are specially built to transport containers–steel boxes that come in standard sizes. These are easy to move, quick to stack and can be filled with all sorts of goods. There are over 20 million containers in the world!

EXTREME ENGINEERING!

The RRS *Sir David Attenborough* is a polar research ship. It's an ice-breaker and its job is to take scientists on Arctic and Antarctic voyages, where they will carry out experiments to study changes in Earth's oceans, sea life and climate.

The ship has a moon pool in its center. This is a vertical shaft, which makes it easy for scientific equipment to be lifted safely into and out of the sea.

The bridge wings let the crew see beyond the sides of the ship to help with maneuvering the ship.

When people move from one country to another, their belongings and furniture are often shipped there inside a container.

The shape of the hull has been designed to fit as many containers on it as possible. The biggest container ships can carry up to 14,500 containers.

Propellers for container ships can be over 33 feet (10 m) wide.

The space inside the ship is divided into sections by bulkheads. So if the hull suffers damage, water only fills that part of the hull and the ship stays afloat.

Container ships need very big, powerful engines to move very heavy loads.

BOATS

Boats are usually smaller than ships. Sailing, rowing, whale watching, canoeing down white water rapids, fishing and breaking a world speed record are just some of their many, many uses.

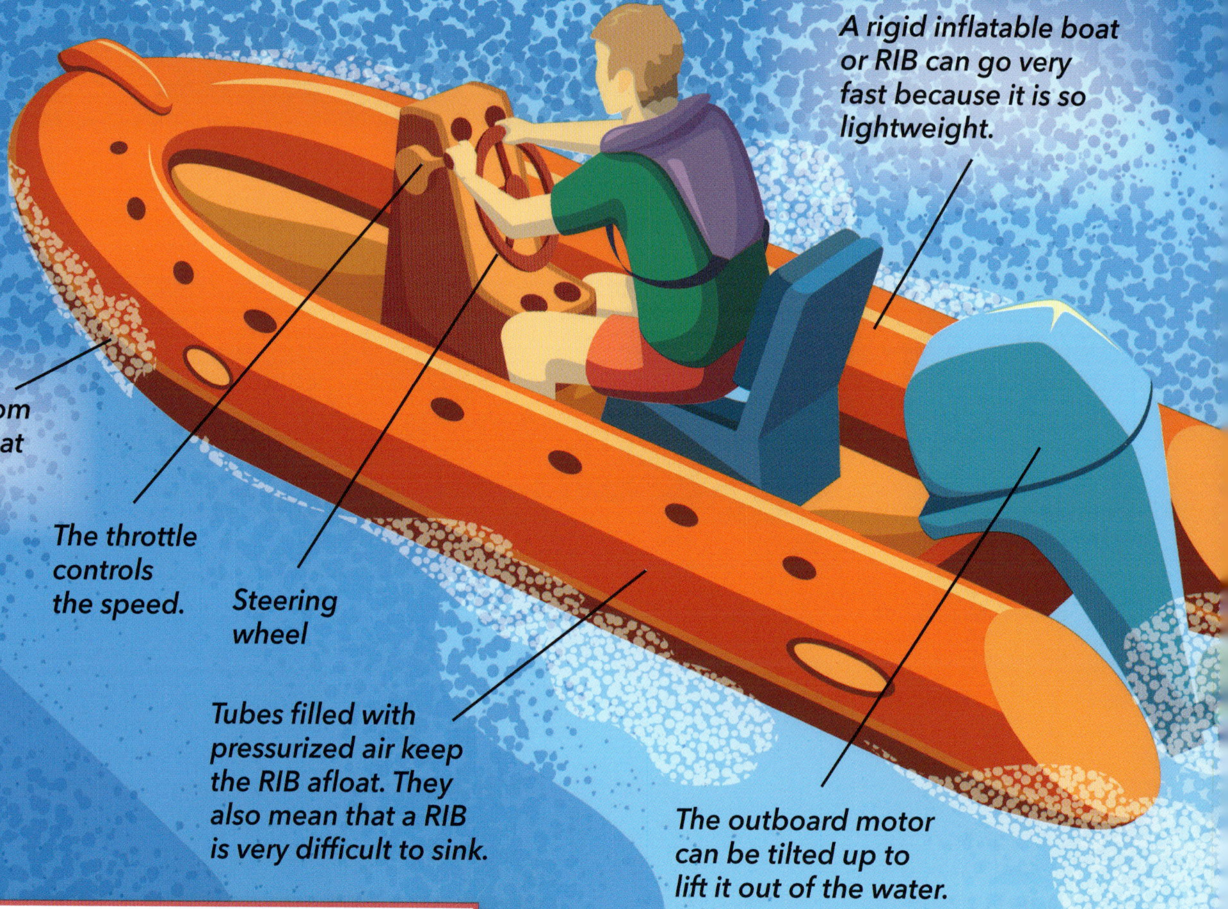

ROUND AND ROUND

The oldest known boat in the world dates back to about 8,000 BCE and was found in a peat bog in the Netherlands. But boats were probably invented much longer ago than this. Early boats would have been powered by humans with a pole, paddle or rope. Later, sails meant that boats could use wind power to go faster and further.

The Pesse canoe is 10 feet (3 m) long and made from a dug-out wooden log.

DIPPING A MOTOR IN THE WATER

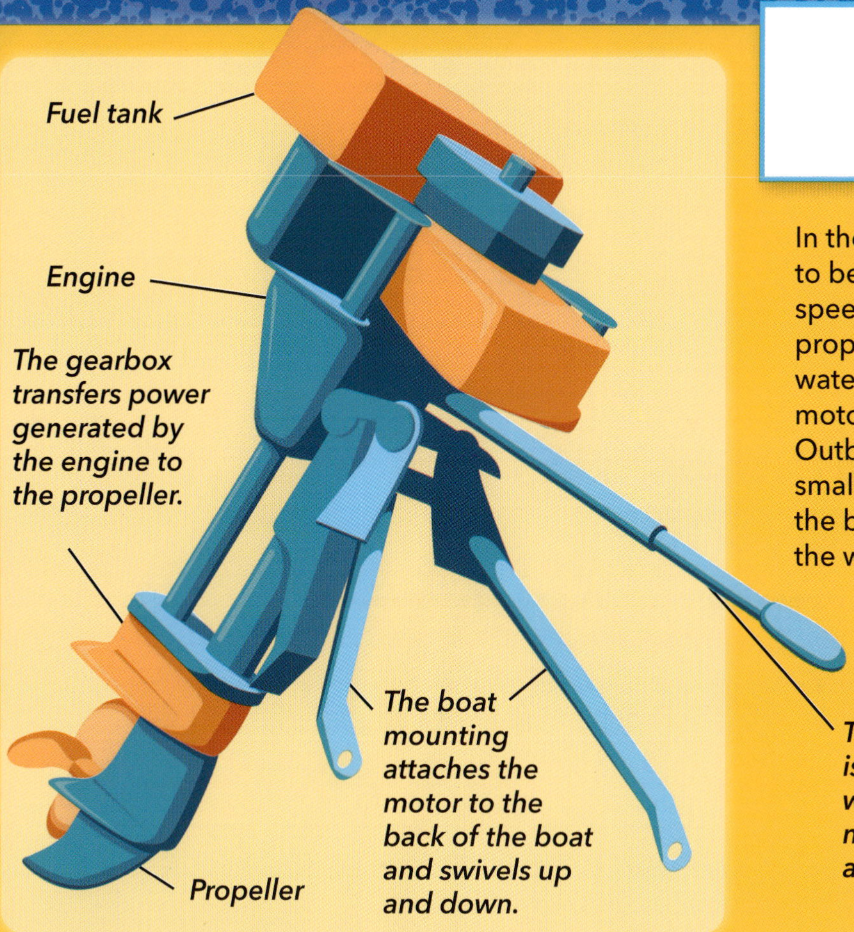

In the 19th century, engines began to be used to make boats even speedier. A boat's engine makes a propeller spin, pushing it through the water. A motorboat has an onboard motor–it's built into the boat. Outboard motors are often fitted to smaller boats. These are attached to the back of a boat and dipped into the water before they are started.

EXTREME ENGINEERING!

In 2018, the Mercury Marine Pyramid set a new world record when they became the largest human waterskiing pyramid ever. Amazingly, the 80-waterskier-pyramid was towed behind just one boat.

The boat was equipped with three powerful Mercury Racing outboard motors.

Some say that the difference between a ship and a boat is that a boat can be put on a ship, but not the other way around.

HOVERCRAFT

A hovercraft travels on a cushion of air. It's amphibious, meaning that it doesn't just whizz over water–it can move over land too. Hovercraft are very good at reaching difficult-to-access places.

IS IT A BOAT, IS IT AN AIRPLANE OR IS IT A HELICOPTER?

A hovercraft is actually a mixture of three different vehicles. It can travel over water like a boat; it is propelled forwards like an airplane; and it hovers like a helicopter. They are often used as ferries as they can easily land on a shoreline, with no need for a harbor.

Hovercraft work by sitting on a cushion of air. Engines power fans that blow air downwards, which pushes the hovercraft upwards. A flexible curtain—called a skirt—hangs around the edge of the hovercraft, to stop all the air escaping. Finally, a propeller at the back of the hovercraft spins to push the vehicle forwards.

This rescue hovercraft is traveling over snow-covered ice.

A hovercraft is also known as an ACV, which stands for air-cushion vehicle.

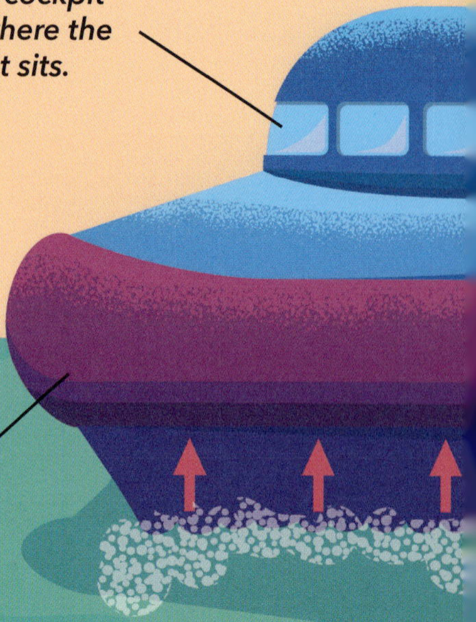

The cockpit is where the pilot sits.

Because the hovercraft sits on a cushion of air, passengers enjoy a smooth ride.

EXTREME ENGINEERING!

Military hovercraft are designed to transport soldiers and supplies to and from difficult-to-reach places. They are ideal for whizzing between sea and shore. They are also the perfect way to zoom over sand, snow and ice.

The US Navy LCAC (Landing Craft Air Cushion) can travel for 370 miles (595 km) without refueling.

HYDROFOILS

Hydrofoils are fast, stable and used around the world. But have you ever wondered how these amazing boats lift themselves out of the water to zoom above the waves? The secret lies beneath the surface ...

Alexander Graham Bell famously invented the telephone. But he also built one of the first hydrofoils. Here, the HD-4 (his fourth hydrofoil) whizzes across a Canadian lake in 1919.

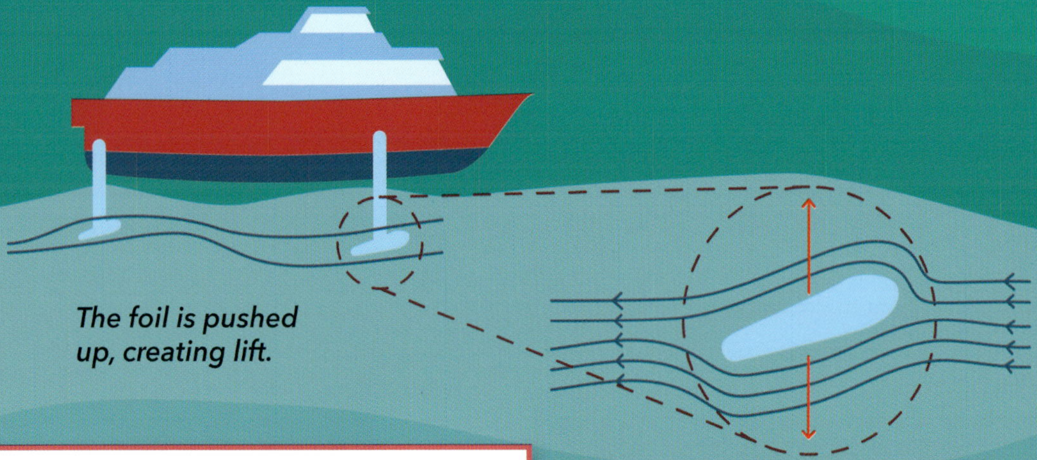

The foil is pushed up, creating lift.

The water flow is pushed down as it goes over the hydrofoil.

WATER WINGS

Hydrofoil isn't just the name of the boat. It also refers to the structures found beneath the boat itself. They are wings that are fixed to the hull and they work like the wings on an airplane. The front of the wing is tilted slightly upwards, so when the boat moves forwards, water is forced downwards. This lifts the boat upwards.

As the hydrofoil travels faster, it lifts higher and higher until the hull is above the surface. This reduces drag—as the boat no longer has to push through the water—allowing the hydrofoil to move much quicker.

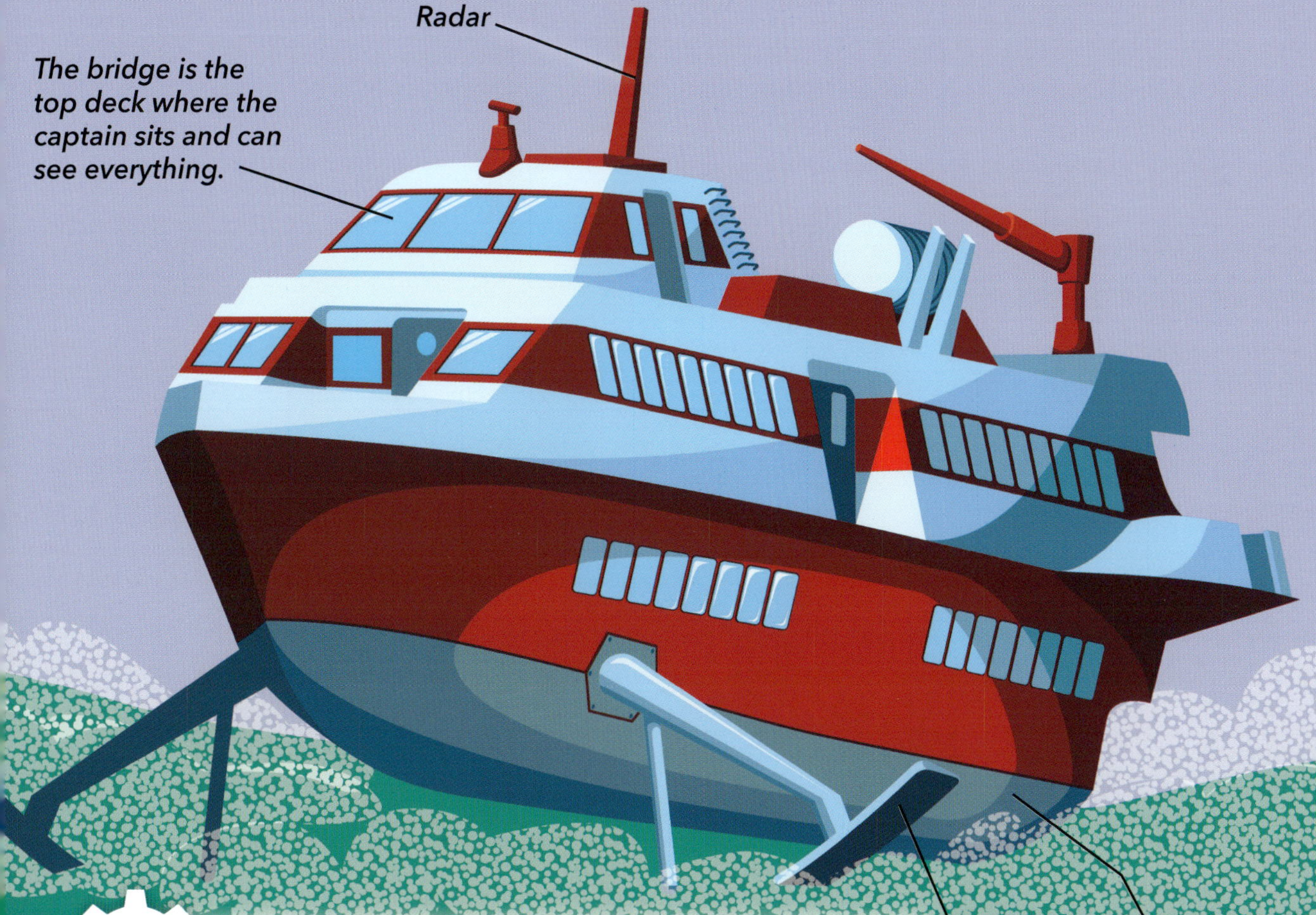

EXTREME ENGINEERING!

Waves are not a problem for the Foiler, which is also known as the "flying yacht." When the water is choppy, its hydrofoils move up and down to ride the waves, while the boat itself stays steady.

ENATA Marine's Foiler is a hybrid—it uses both diesel and electric engines.

CATAMARANS

Catamarans have two hulls instead of one. Some have sails, some have engines and some have both. Larger catamarans are often used as ferries, while smaller catamarans are very popular in sailing. Catamarans have even been used for round-the-world voyages.

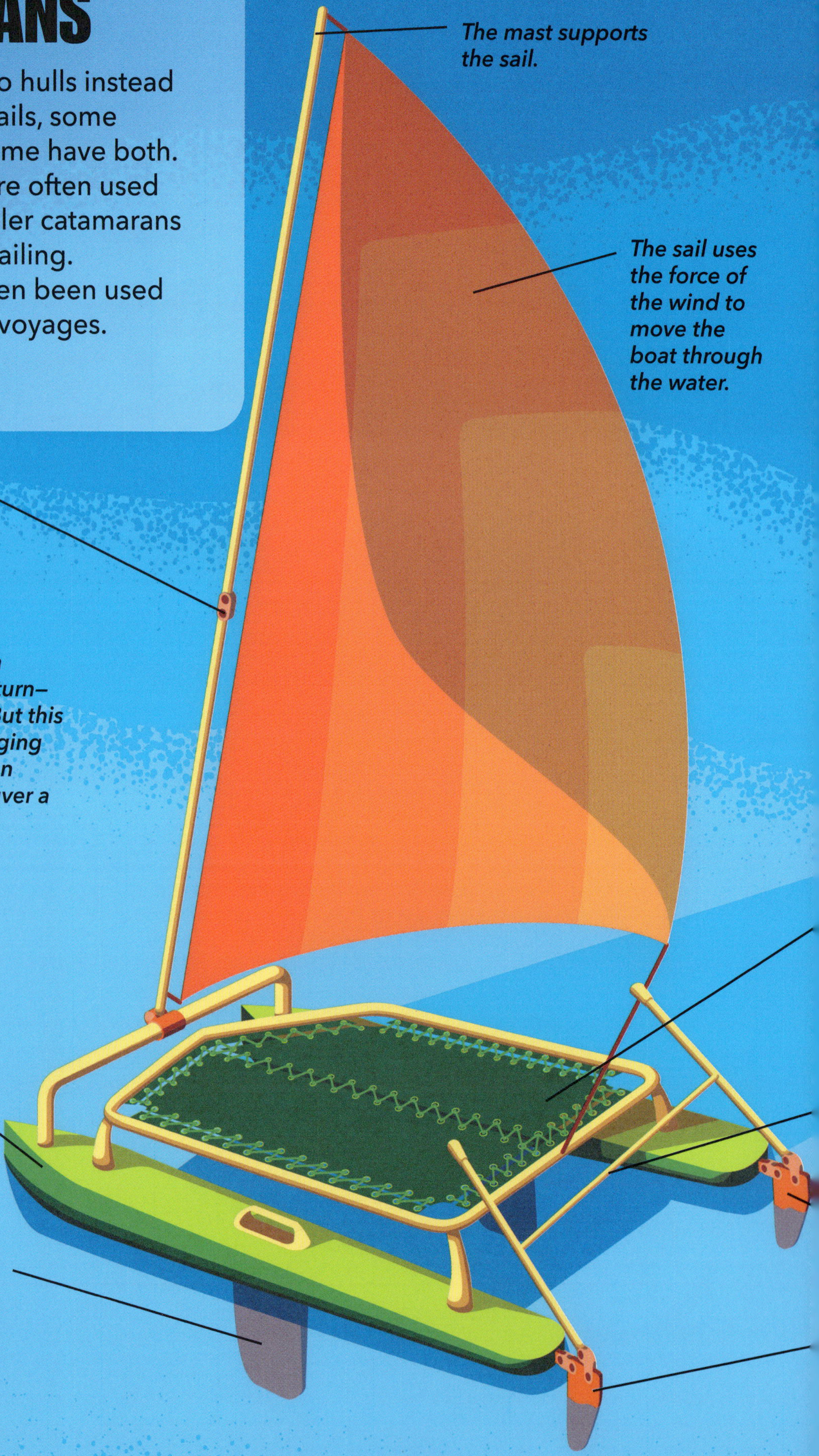

The mast supports the sail.

The sail uses the force of the wind to move the boat through the water.

The rigging is a system of cables, ropes and pulleys used to hoist and control the sail.

It is more difficult for a catamaran to tack–or turn–because it's so wide. But this makes it more challenging during races. It takes an expert sailor to maneuver a catamaran at speed!

During races, one of the catamaran's hulls often lifts right out of the water!

A catamaran has a daggerboard or keel in each hull. They are used to keep the boat steady in the water. They can be removed to stop them scraping the seabed in shallow waters.

WHEN TWO HULLS GO TO SEA

Catamarans have two narrow hulls connected by a wide beam, which means they are far less likely to rock from side to side than a single-hulled boat. (To understand why catamarans are more stable, stand with your feet apart. Now stand on one leg. Which feels wobblier?) Catamarans make great ferries because they are stable even in choppy seas.

A bigger sail means a faster boat. So, because the hulls of a catamaran are spaced apart, there's room to have a bigger sail than on a normal boat, which increases speed. As the twin hulls are narrow, they slice through the water making the catamaran go faster still.

The catamaran is not a new invention. These boats were first sailed by the Polynesians 3,500 years ago.

Pieces of strong fabric are stretched between the hulls. This flat area where sailors can sit is called a trampoline.

The tiller links the two rudders together so they move at the same time.

The rudders are used for steering.

EXTREME ENGINEERING!

Launched in 2013, Incat's HSC *Francisco* is a super-fast ferry, shaped to cut through the water. But as well as being quick and large—with room for 1,000 passengers and 150 cars—it's also environmentally friendly. The catamaran links Buenos Aires, Argentina and Montevideo, Uruguay.

HSC Francisco has a top speed of 58 knots (66.5 mph, 107 kph).

AIRCRAFT CARRIERS

An aircraft carrier is a warship that does exactly what its name suggests—it carries aircraft. But it doesn't just do this. An aircraft carrier also has a flight deck so the aircraft can take off and land. It's a runway at sea!

The General R Ford (CVN-78) is a nuclear-powered aircraft carrier with space for 75 aircraft.

UP, UP AND AWAY!

Aircraft carriers are mobile military air bases that transport aircraft to wherever they need to be. There's room for hundreds or even thousands of crew on board. But even though these ships can be huge, the flight deck is still much shorter than a normal runway. This is not a problem for helicopters (which use VTOL—vertical take off and landing) or tiltrotors (which use either VTOL or STOL—short take off and landing). But fixed-wing aircraft need a helping hand to take off and land.

Some aircraft carriers have a ramp at the end of the flight deck. The ramp angles fighter jets upwards so that when they take off, they climb into the sky instead of falling into the sea. Many jets dangle a tailhook beneath them when they come in to land. The tailhook snags on steel wires stretched across the deck. A hydraulic system attached to the wires slows planes down gradually, but also quickly.

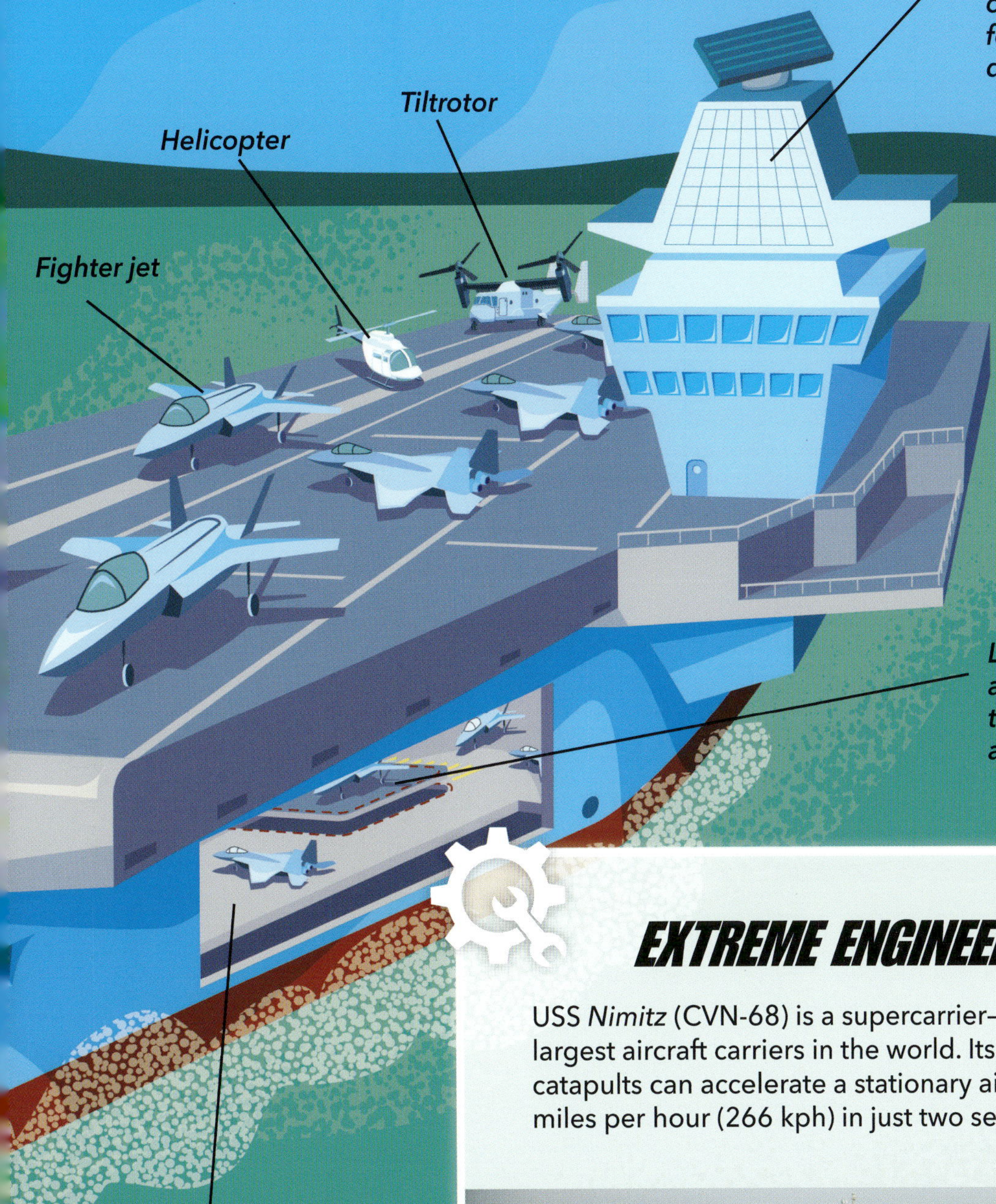

EXTREME ENGINEERING!

USS *Nimitz* (CVN-68) is a supercarrier–one of the largest aircraft carriers in the world. Its steam-powered catapults can accelerate a stationary aircraft to 165 miles per hour (266 kph) in just two seconds.

Nimitz's two nuclear reactors power four main engines giving the ship a top speed of over 30 knots, or 34 mph (55 kph).

PERSONAL WATERCRAFT

Personal watercraft are like motorcycles, but they whizz over water instead of roads. These small, speedy machines made for one or two (although sometimes there's room for more) are often known by their brand names, such as Jet Ski®, WaveRunner® and Sea-Doo®.

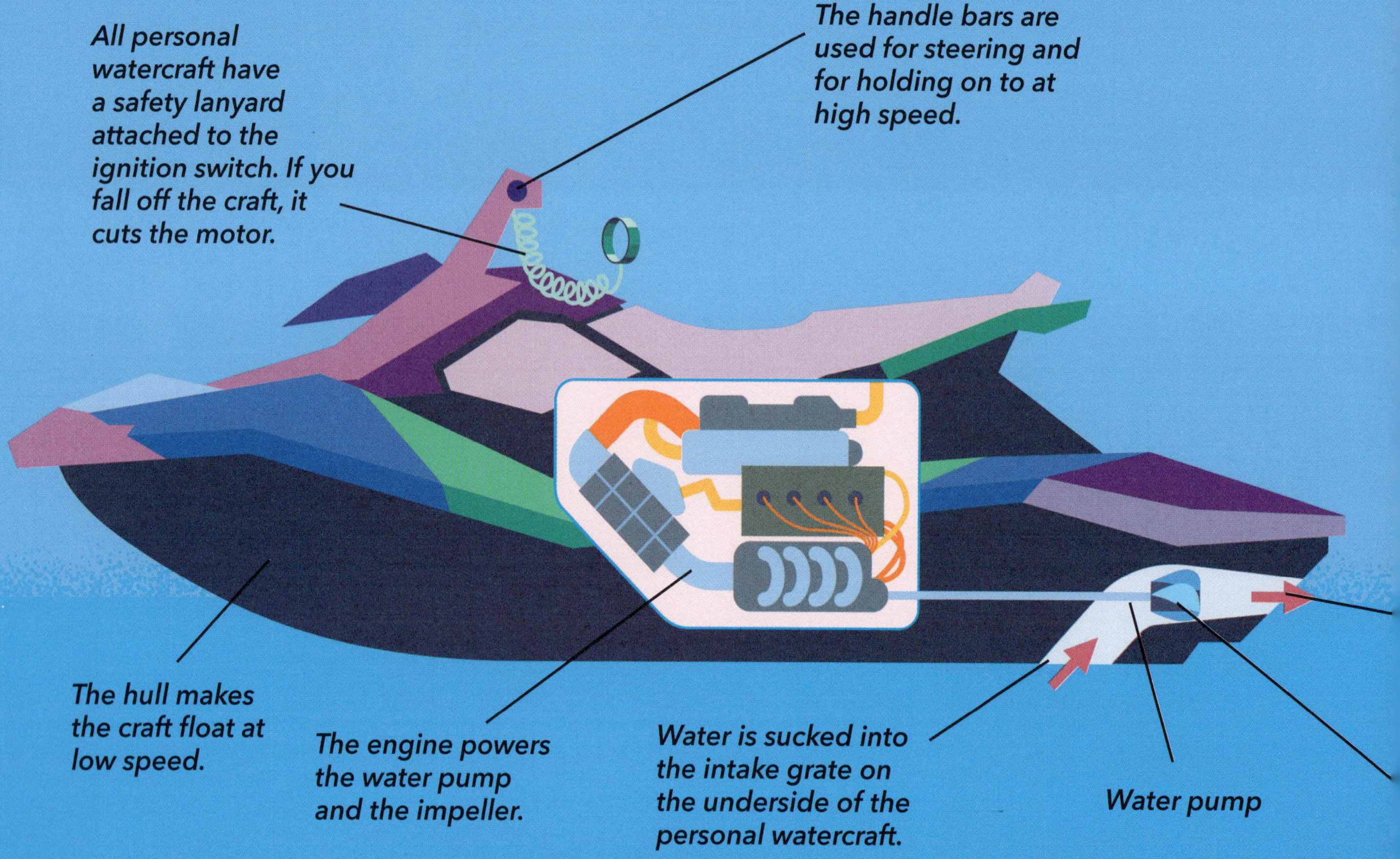

WHOOSH!

Early personal watercraft were used by a single passenger, who stood up and held on to handlebars. Later designs were more like motorcycles, with a saddle and room for passengers. These machines are so powerful that they can leap out of the water. Some can even do somersaults!

Personal watercraft are powered by an onboard engine. The engine runs a water pump, called an impeller—a propeller fitted into a pipe inside the watercraft. When the impeller spins, it sucks water into the bottom of the watercraft and pushes it out of a nozzle at the back. When this jet of water is forced backwards, the watercraft moves forwards. Turning the handlebars changes the direction of the nozzle, which changes the direction of the watercraft!

The steering nozzle is smaller than the water intake, and that's what builds up the water speed.

The impeller has three blades.

EXTREME ENGINEERING!

The Zapata Flyride™ can actually fly. Instead of one jet of water, this personal watercraft actually has three. The water jet at the back of the vehicle powers it up into the air. The jets on the right and left are used to steer.

At the touch of a button the Zapata Flyride™ can even perform a barrel roll!

SEAPLANES

Wilbur and Orville Wright designed and built the first airplane–the *Wright Flyer*–in 1903. But airplanes needed runways. And as these were so rare, the race was on to invent an aircraft that could land on a flat surface that was much more common–the sea.

Floatplanes are perfect for traveling the short distance between the city of Vancouver and Vancouver Island in British Columbia, Canada.

IS IT A PLANE OR IS IT A BOAT?

There are different types of seaplane. A floatplane is a light aircraft that has long, narrow pontoons–or floats–instead of standard landing gear. The floats make the aircraft heavier, less aerodynamic and slower, so floatplanes are usually used for short journeys and carry few passengers. Meanwhile, a flying boat is less like an aircraft and more like a boat with wings. The hull touches down onto the water.

Floatplanes always have overhead wings - to keep them out of the way of the water.

A flying boat

When landing gear is added to a floatplane or a flying boat, it becomes an amphibious aircraft. This means it can touch down on land or water!

Seaplanes fly in the same way as fixed-wing aircraft. Engines provide power and wings create lift. It's their ability to take off from water and land on water that makes seaplanes different.

EXTREME ENGINEERING!

A FlyShip® is a mixture of aircraft and boat. It saves energy—and fuel—by relying on ground effect. This is the extra lift that aircraft wings experience when they fly very close to the ground ... or the sea.

Traveling by FlyShip® promises to be much faster than traveling by boat.

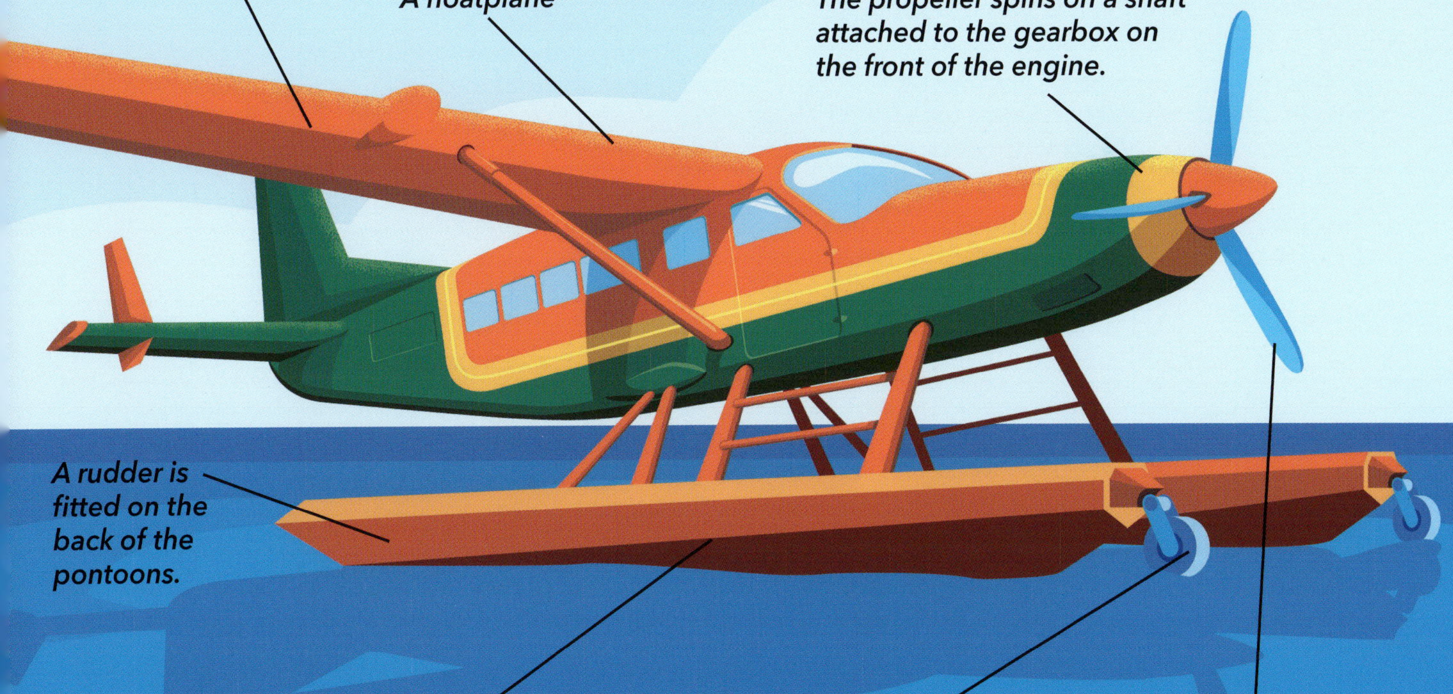

SUBMARINES

It's not easy to hide a ship and in wartime they are obvious targets for the enemy. But submarines are different. Once they dive beneath the waves, it's difficult to track them. They can surprise the enemy. And they can stay underwater for months ...

Submarines are tube-shaped with rounded ends, so they can glide smoothly through the water

INSIDE THE SUBMARINE

Submarines usually have two hulls. The outer hull is a non-watertight shell, shaped to glide easily through water. Meanwhile, the watertight inner hull—inside which the crew lives and works—is made of super strong steel or titanium to resist water pressure, which increases the deeper the vessel goes into the sea. Ballast tanks between the two hulls are flooded with water to make the submarine sink. When compressed air is blown into the tanks, this pushes out the water and the submarine rises to the surface.

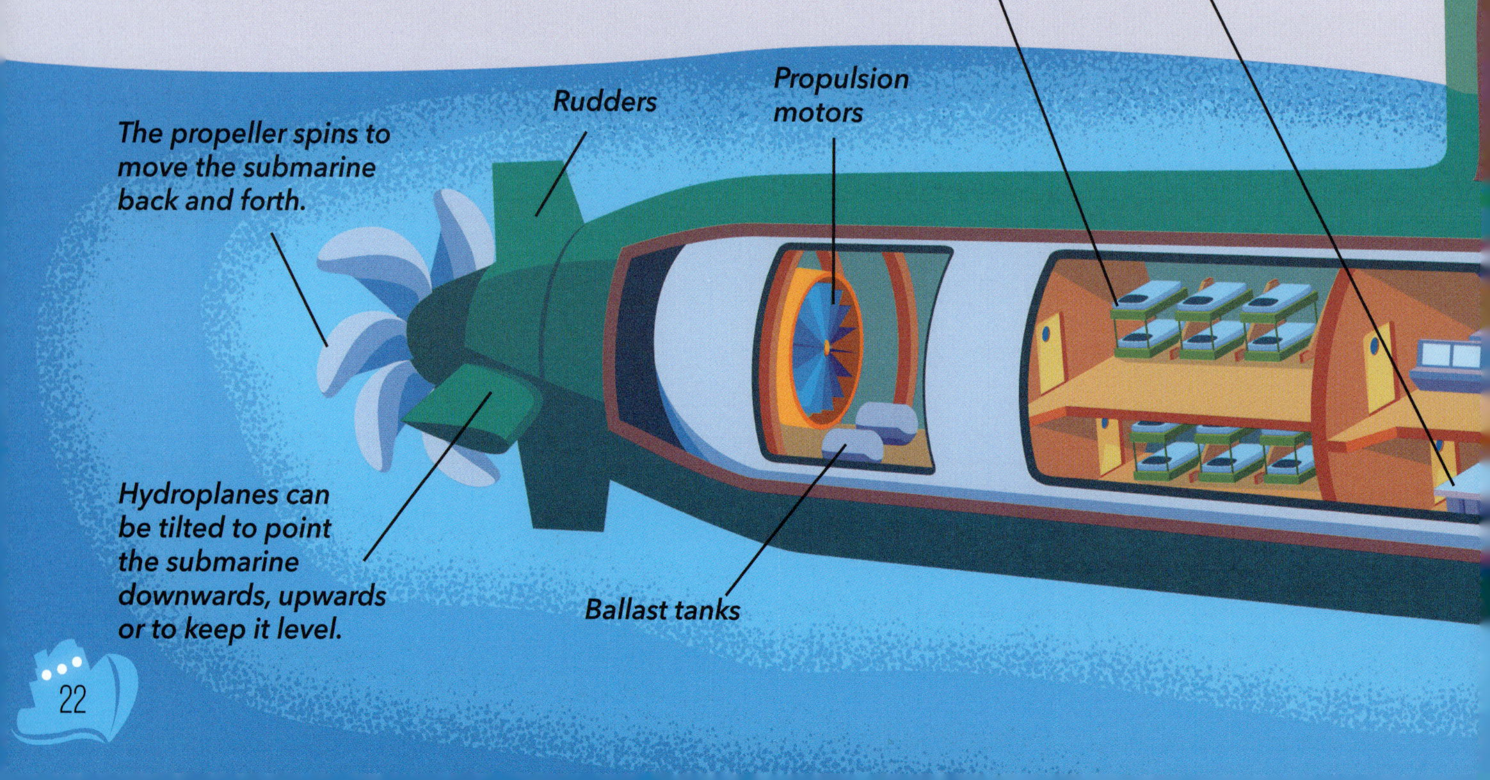

SUBMARINE POWER

Submarines need power for two reasons–to make the vessel move and to run all the equipment inside. In diesel submarines, the diesel engines need oxygen to work, so these are run when the submarine is above water, charging the batteries on board. These batteries are used to power the vessel when it's underwater, but the submarine must surface regularly to recharge them. In nuclear submarines, power is provided by nuclear reactors. Because these do not need oxygen to run, the submarine can stay underwater for months at a time.

EXTREME ENGINEERING!

Astute class nuclear submarines can run for 25 years before refueling. They are also the quietest submarines ever built. This makes them perfect for secret missions ... Shhh.

Astute class submarines are built in Barrow-in-Furness, Cumbria in the UK.

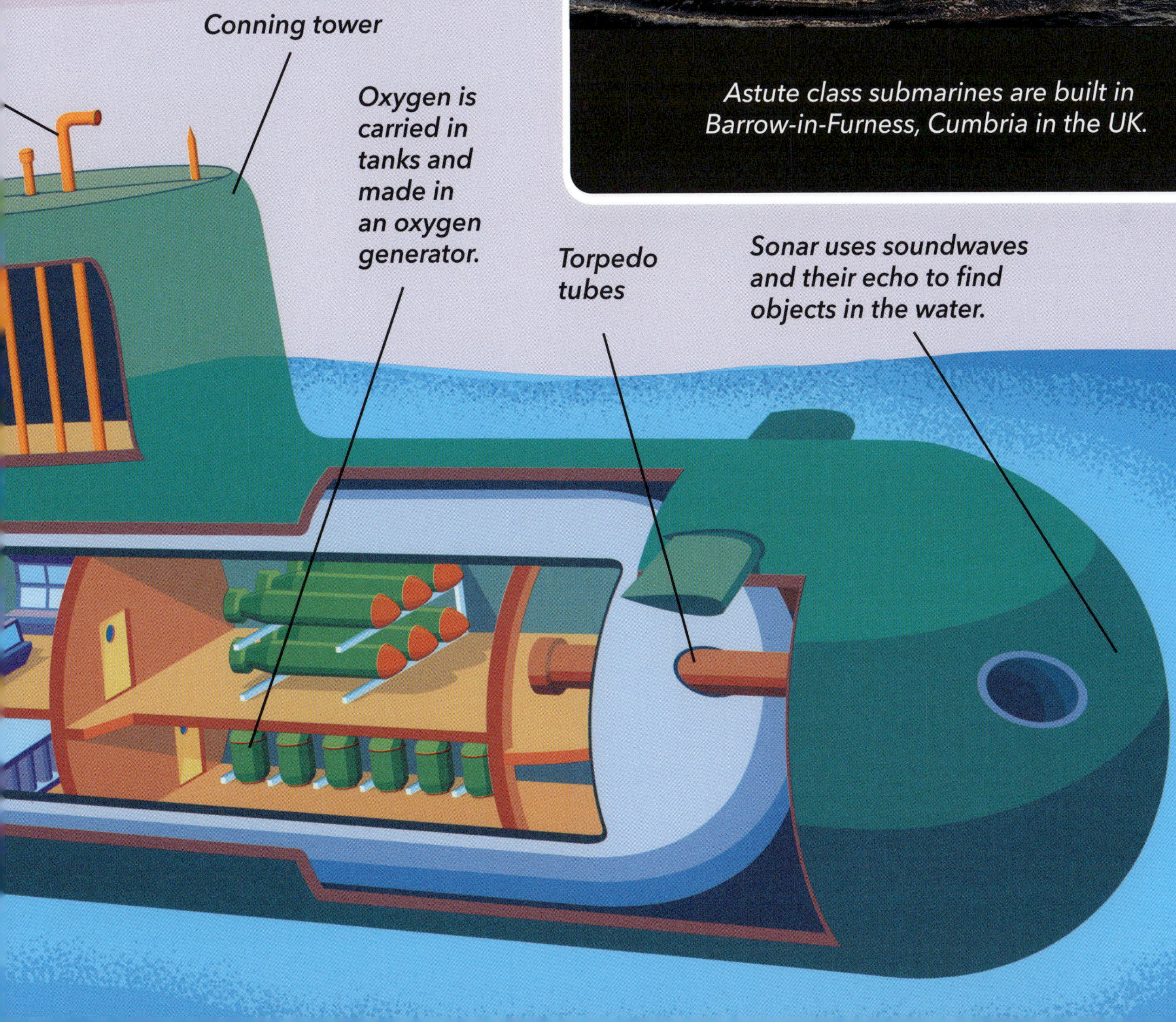

SUBMERSIBLES

A submersible is like a submarine, but much smaller. Sometimes, it's crewed by just one person. And while a submarine can operate entirely on its own, a submersible relies on a support team at the surface. These tiny craft are often used for underwater research and exploration.

The Triton 3300/3 can take three people to a depth of 3,281 feet (1,000 m).

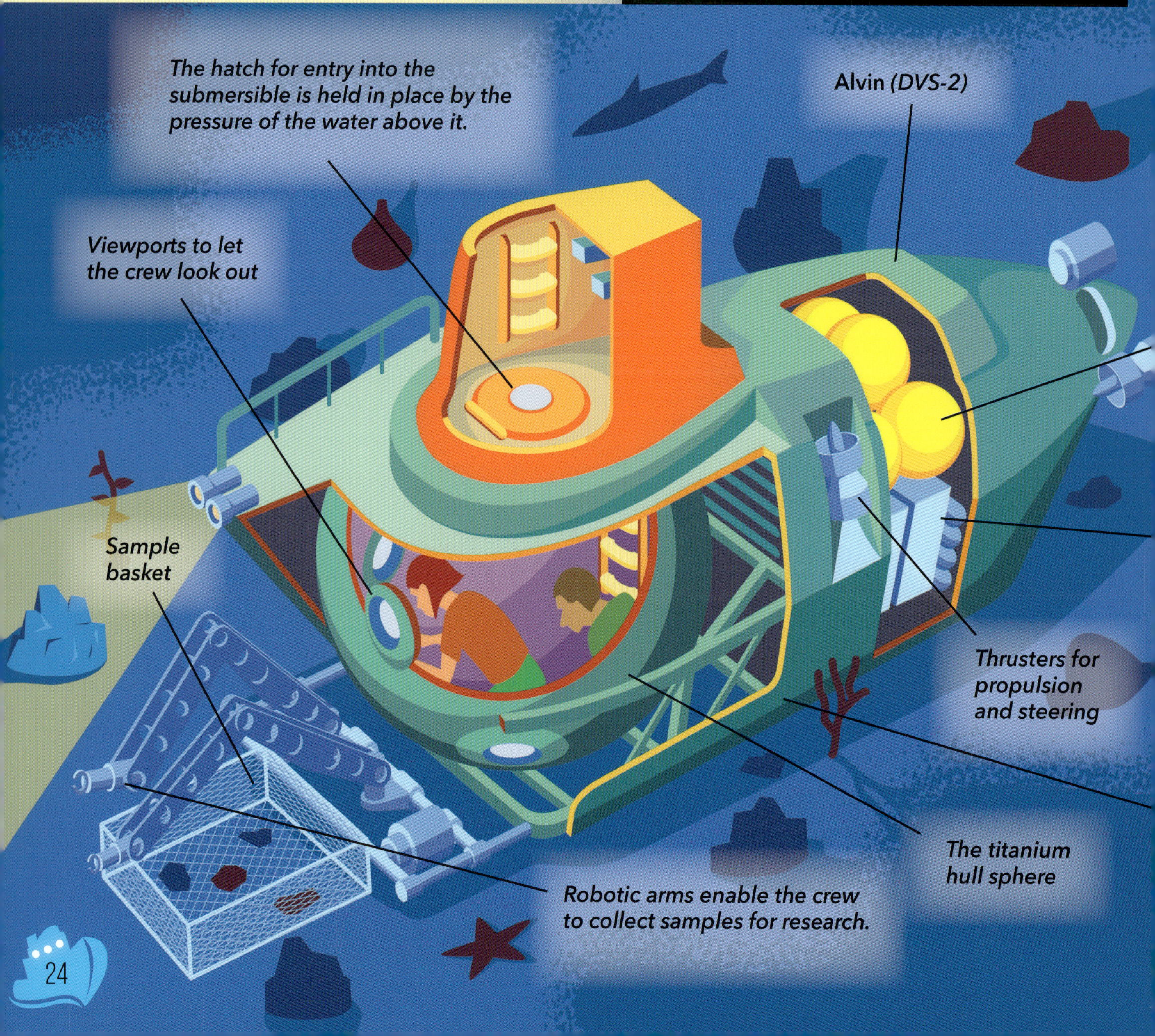

EXPLORING THE OCEAN

There are different types of submersible. Remotely operated vehicles (ROVs) are attached, or tethered, to a vessel on the surface by a cable. This cable provides power to the ROV, while communicating data back to the surface. It is also used to recover the ROV (haul it back to ship). An autonomous underwater vehicle (AUV) does not use a cable at all and supplies its own power. Un-crewed submersibles are perfect for dives that are too deep or too risky for humans.

Alvin (DSV-2) is a research submersible with room for a pilot and two scientists. The newest model has a titanium sphere to protect those inside from the water pressure at extreme depths. The submersible is fitted with steel weights that allow it to dive quickly. These are left on the seabed after each dive. *Alvin* has dived thousands of times. Once, it explored the wreck of RMS *Titanic*!

Ballast and air pressure spheres to help with buoyancy and stability

Batteries and control equipment for power and utilities

Descent weights are dropped on the seabed so the submersible is light enough to return to the surface.

EXTREME ENGINEERING!

In 1960, Jacques Piccard and Don Walsh traveled to the bottom of the Marianas Trench in the western Pacific Ocean in a bathyscaphe—a free-diving submersible. The *Trieste* flooded air tanks with seawater to sink, then dumped its iron pellet ballast to go up again. At such depths, buoyancy is not provided by air but by tanks filled with gas.

The bathyscaphe Trieste dived 35,797 feet (10,911 m) under the surface of the Pacific Ocean to reach the deepest place on Earth.

DIVING GEAR

Submersibles allow people to look at the underwater world, but diving equipment means that they can go even closer. SCUBA stands for self-contained underwater breathing apparatus. It gives divers the freedom to explore the underwater world themselves.

BREATHING UNDERWATER

SCUBA gear allows divers to breathe underwater. As a tank of air would be used up very quickly, the air is compressed, or squeezed, to fit in as much as possible. Every time the diver takes a breath, a regulator reduces the pressure of the compressed air to a normal, breathable level.

There are two ways of dealing with the gases a diver breathes out. With open-circuit demand SCUBA, the air bubbles away into the sea. But with rebreather SCUBA, the air is cleaned, recycled and topped up with oxygen from the tank.

EXTREME ENGINEERING!

Atmospheric diving suits allow divers to go deeper than ever. Nuytco Research Ltd's Exosuit is made of metal and packed with equipment. During a dive, the pressure remains the same as it is on the surface. This means there is no danger of a diver becoming ill if they go up to the surface too quickly.

The Jet Suit 3 is powered by five kerosene-fuelled micro gas turbines–two on each arm and one on the back.

MORE MAGNIFICENT MACHINES

Symphony of the Seas is almost as long as four football fields.

ROYAL CARIBBEAN'S *SYMPHONY OF THE SEAS*

Millions of people go on cruises every year. So the newest cruise ships are growing bigger and bigger to make sure there is enough room for them. Royal Caribbean's *Symphony of the Seas* (launched in 2017) has 18 decks and measures 1,184 feet (361 m) from bow to stern. It can hold up to 6,680 passengers and 2,200 crew.

AIRBOAT

Marshlands are too wet and swampy for cars, yet the water is too shallow and full of reeds for most boats. But they are the perfect place for airboats. These flat-bottomed boats are not powered by normal boat engines, which dip a small propeller into the water. Instead, a large propeller sits on top of the boat to push through the air. An airboat is so small and its engine and propeller so big that it can travel at speeds of over 93 mph (150 kph).

Airboats are often used as rescue boats during floods.

DAZZLE SHIPS

During World War I (1914–18) and World War II (1939–45), many ships were painted with complicated colorful patterns. Dazzle designs made it difficult to work out how far away the ships were, their speed and their direction. In 2014, German artist Tobias Rehberger gave HMS *President* (1918), which was originally a dazzle ship, a new lease of life by covering it entirely in his "reimagining" of the original dazzle style.

The patterns on dazzle ships were designed to confuse the enemy.

TAMAR CLASS LIFEBOAT

Rescuing people from rough seas can be very dangerous. This is why lifeboats are designed to be as safe as possible. The Tamar class lifeboat uses an electronic system that means crew can operate the boat's many features without leaving their shock-absorbing seats!

The Tamar class lifeboat is self-righting–if it capsizes, it flips the right way up again!

GLOSSARY

amphibious
relating to vehicles that can move both on land and in water

barrel roll
a complete roll to the left or the right, while the object continues in a forward direction

bridge
the raised part of a ship on which the captain and other officers stand and from where they control the movement of the ship

ballast tank
used to help a submersible and submarine sink or float

bulkhead
a wall that divides the inside of a ship or aircraft

buoyancy
an object's ability to float

capsize
to cause a boat or ship to turn upside down by accident while on water

cargo
goods carried by a vehicle such as a ship

catamaran
a boat with two hulls

compressed
squeezed

drag
the force that acts against the forward movement of something

funnel
a metal chimney on a ship or steam engine

hull
the main body of a ship; the part that sits in the water

hybrid
something made by combining features of two other things

hydraulic
when something is operated using a liquid

hydroplane
a fin-like attachment that enables a moving submarine to rise or fall in the water

ice breaker
a ship designed for breaking through ice

lift
the upward force applied on the wing of a bird or aircraft that keeps it in the air as it moves forwards

knots
a measure of the speed of ships, aircraft, or movements of water and air

maneuver
to turn an object and make it go where you want

merchant ship
a vessel that is used to carry cargo

navigation
working out where a vessel is and where it's going

pressure
when something pushes against something else

propeller
a device that spins to move a boat or an aircraft

propulsion
a force that pushes something forwards

radar
a system that uses radio waves to find the position of objects that cannot be seen

regulator
a device that controls the flow of gases breathed by a diver

shaft
a narrow, vertical hole

sonar
equipment, especially on a ship, that uses sound waves to discover how deep the water is or the position of an object in the water

polar
relating to the North or South Pole or the areas around them

Polynesians
the people of Polynesia, a region of the central Pacific

pontoon
each of a pair of floats fitted to an aircraft to enable it to land on water

submersible
a craft that operates under water

tailhook
device attached to the tail of some military fixed-wing aircraft. The hook is used to quickly slow down the aircraft so it can land aboard an aircraft carrier's flight deck at sea

titanium
a light, strong, white metal

torpedo
a long, thin bomb that travels underwater in order to destroy the ship at which it is aimed

WEBSITES

Find out about the National Maritime Museum in London.
rmg.co.uk/national-maritime-museum

Find out more about the Royal Navy Submarine Museum in Gosport.
nmrn.org.uk/submarine-museum

Take a virtual tour of the Science Museum's Shipping collection.
sciencemuseum.org.uk/what-was-on/shipping#virtual-tour

Dive back in time with the US National Maritime Historical Society's "Sea History for Kids" website.
seahistory.org/kids-category/vessels/

Discover the Tall Ships Round UK Youth Sailing Challenge.
tallships.org

BOOKS

Boats: Fast & Slow
by Iris Volant and Jarom Vogel (Nobrow Press, 2018)

Exploring Science: Ships & Boats
by Chris Oxlade (Armadillo Books, 2015)

Ultimate Military Machines: Submarines
by Tim Cooke (Wayland, 2018)

What's Inside: Submarines
by David West (Franklin Watts, 2016)

Cars, Trains, Ships & Planes (DK, 2015)

Children's Transport Encyclopedia
by Philip Wilkinson, Oliver Green & Ian Graham (QED Publishing, 2016)

INDEX